Big Belching Bog

Big Belching Bog

Phyllis Root

Illustrations by Betsy Bowen

University of Minnesota Press
Minneapolis · London

Published by the University of Minnesota Press
111 Third Avenue South, Suite 290
Minneapolis, MN 55401-2520
http://www.upress.umn.edu

A Cataloging-in-Publication record is available from the Library of Congress.
ISBN: 978-0-8166-6682-9 (pb)

Printed in China on acid-free paper

30 29 28 27 26 25 24 23   10 9 8 7 6 5 4 3 2 1

To Kelly, friend and fellow traveler
 —P.R.

To Hermi the hermit thrush
 —B.B.

If you come to the Big Bog
you might think you have come
to the loneliest, quietest place on earth.

In the flat bed of a long-gone glacial lake,
rain drains so slowly
you can hardly see it flow.

Sphagnum moss many feet deep blankets the bog,
turning the water brown and acidic,
keeping it icy
well into summer.

If you come to the Big Bog
go slowly
(you can't hurry a bog)
and listen.
The bog might share some of its secrets with you.
You might even hear the biggest bog secret of all.

Plants that grow in the big blooming bog
have their own secrets to survive.
Labrador tea plants keep their same leaves
    year after year,
saving the energy it would take
    to grow new ones.
Leatherleaf curls its thick leaves down
to keep from losing water.
Stemless lady's slippers
unfolding like tiny pink moccasins
get food from the fungi around their roots.

Mosquitoes buzz in the big buggy bog.
Horseflies, too, and little black flies.
But here's a bog secret:
some plants in the bog eat insects.
Round-leaved sundews trap them
    in their sticky leaves,
which slowly close.

Flies that fall into pitcher plant pitchers
drown in the water at the bottom.
Here's another bog secret:
some insects, like the larvae
   of the pitcher plant mosquitoes,
live inside pitcher plants
   and never get eaten.

And deep in the peat,
down below pitcher plants,
sundews,
and buzzing mosquitoes,
something
is growing,
pushing,
heading your way.

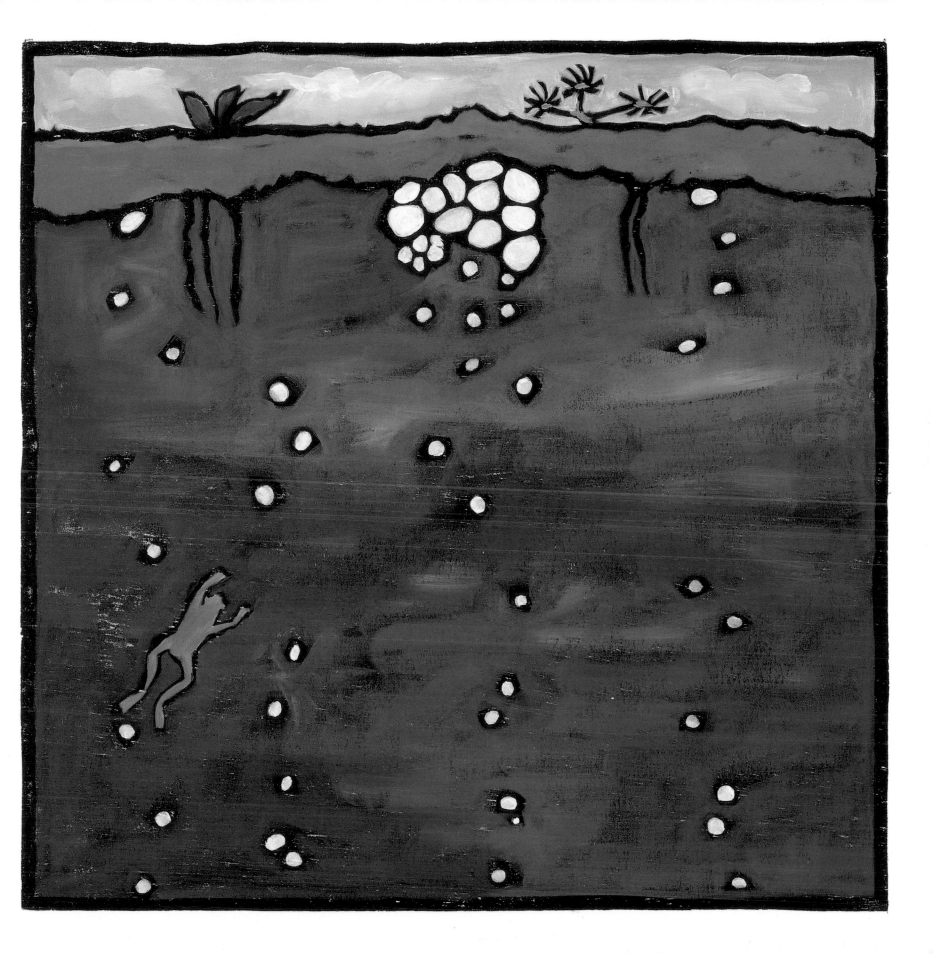

You might think all sorts of toads and frogs
would live in the watery bog,
but most of their eggs won't hatch in the acid water.
Wood frogs are bog frogs, and they survive.
Here's a secret about frogs in winter:
a kind of antifreeze in their bodies
lets them stay frozen alive
until spring thaws them out again.

Butterflies that flit from bog flower to bog flower
have their own secrets, too.
Bog copper butterfly eggs
wait all winter on cranberry leaves.
Once they hatch into caterpillars,
they wait the next winter, too,
before making their chrysalises and emerging
to brighten the bog with their wings.

And while butterflies flitter and feed,
under the creeping cranberries,
under the bog rosemary
something is rising, rising,
heading your way.

More than one hundred different species of birds
come to the Big Bog or live here year round.
Some birds are hidden deep in the bog
so you might not see them at all.
But palm warblers waggle their tails here,
and sandhill cranes raise their chicks.
If you listen you might hear
black-backed woodpeckers hammering
or a hermit thrush shivering the air with song.

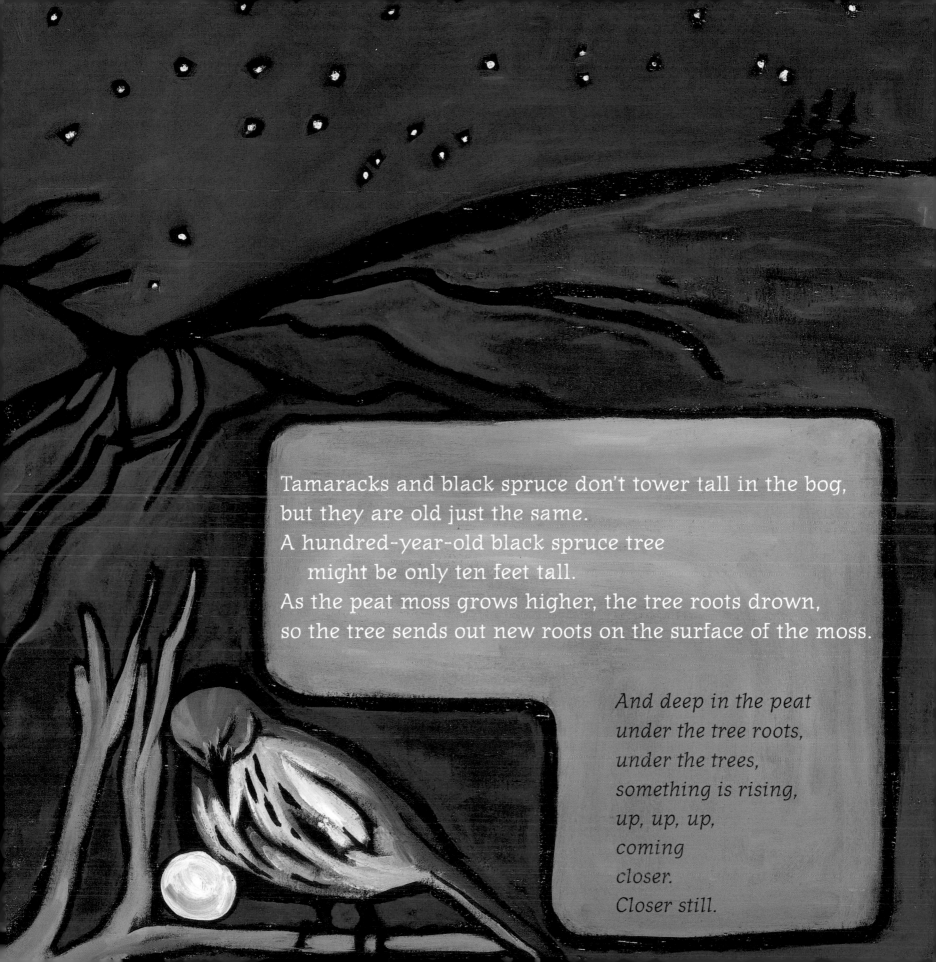

Tamaracks and black spruce don't tower tall in the bog,
but they are old just the same.
A hundred-year-old black spruce tree
    might be only ten feet tall.
As the peat moss grows higher, the tree roots drown,
so the tree sends out new roots on the surface of the moss.

And deep in the peat
under the tree roots,
under the trees,
something is rising,
up, up, up,
coming
closer.
Closer still.

If you put your ear to a hilly hummock of moss
and listen very, very quietly
you might hear a tiny bog lemming
skittering through a tunnel.
You might see small haystacks of sedge clippings
left in the sun to dry for food.
Most burrowers in the bog
live in tiny islands of moss.
Come winter, bog lemmings tunnel under the snow,
out of view from great gray owls hunting.

If you listen carefully,
you might hear a moose trudging by,
hooves sinking into the bouncy bog,
or hear the almost silent footsteps of an eastern gray wolf.
Not many big animals live in the bog,
but they might come to nibble the branches of alder trees
or shelter in bog willow thickets.

No matter how hard you listen, though,
you won't hear the hooves of caribou
(although you might see their ghosts passing through).
Caribou lived in the Big Bog
    before they moved farther north,
leaving their trails in the peat.
The spongy moss holds on to hoof prints
    for a long, long time.

And down below the surface of the bog
that moss is at work,
breaking down,
decaying,
releasing methane gas,
deep down,
but rising, rising.

If you are very lucky in the bog
you might see the surface of the moss bulge up
six inches or more
until

BELCH

The methane gas
belches out.
And the moss sinks
down again.

Does the belching bog make a sound?
This is the biggest bog secret of all.
No one knows.
Scientists are studying the bog to find out,
but no one has ever heard the Big Bog belch.

If you go to the big belching bog,
the big buggy blooming bog
    of butterflies and burrowers and birds,
go slowly
and listen.

You might be the very first person to hear
the big bog
belch.

Bog Facts

A bog is a wetland with a surface made primarily of sphagnum moss. Its waters are poor in minerals. Bogs are found in many countries and on several continents, including Canada, Russia, Sweden, England, Germany, Africa, South America, and Japan. Some bogs form in depressions and old lake beds. Some form by lakes slowly filling in from the edges.

A bog forms when slow-moving or stagnant water keeps plants from breaking down or decaying quickly when they die. As dead plants sink they form a mat of peat that breaks down very slowly and makes the water in the bog more acidic. The peat may be thirty feet deep or more in some bogs.

Bogs preserve other things besides dead plants. In Europe centuries-old tools, pottery, coins, and even bodies have been found in bogs. In Poland a tank that sank during World War II was pulled out almost perfectly preserved from a bog.

The Big Bog in Minnesota is the largest peatland in the lower forty-eight United States. It is in the northwestern part of the state, where Glacial Lake Agassiz, a lake that was bigger than all the Great Lakes put together, once held the water from melting glaciers. When the water drained away, it left a flat lake bed. The only water in the bog comes from rainfall and drains away very slowly. Sphagnum moss grows in this water; as new moss grows, old moss sinks down. This acidic water stays cold well into summer, so many plants cannot grow here. A few plants and trees do grow on and in this mat of dead and living plants. In some bogs only three kinds of trees, ten kinds of shrubs, six kinds of flowers, and six kinds of grasses and sedges survive in the cold, acidic water.

As plants break down in a bog, they create methane gas. This gas slowly rises through the bog until it forces its way out at the surface, making the bog

belch. Scientists warn that a warming planet may dry up bogs and release all the stored methane, which could make global climate change worse.

In Minnesota the Big Bog State Recreation Area has a mile-long boardwalk into the bog. Labrador tea, bog rosemary, and other plants grow along the boardwalk. Sunlight shines through the pitchers of pitcher plants. Tiny red cranberries lie on the moss. Birds flit and call in the tamarack and spruce trees. At the end of the board-walk, islands of trees sail in the distance on a sea of grass and sedge. You are in one of the quietest and wildest places in Minnesota.

Minnesota has many other bogs; some are located in state parks and scientific and natural areas. Other northern states such as Michigan, Maine, New York, and Wisconsin also have many bogs.

If you go to a bog in the spring or sum-mer, bring insect repellent or wear long sleeves and pants to protect yourself from mosquitoes. Be sure to have a com-pass and map with you—it can be easy to get lost when everything around you is flat. Look, listen, but don't take any-thing away with you. Everything in the bog works hard to survive.

Some people look at a bog and think that land should be more useful than it is. Bogs have been filled in so buildings could be built on that site. They have been drained for farming. Peat has been harvested for fuel, and trees have been cut for timber. But bogs are unique eco-systems. Some rare animals live only in bogs. Others come to bogs to raise their young or to rest and eat on their long migration routes. Bogs help to filter water and prevent flooding by holding the water, like a giant sponge. When a bog is drained, disturbed, or destroyed, it is gone forever.

Plants in the Bog

Sphagnum moss *Sphagnum* (many species)

Sphagnum moss is like a giant sponge, holding many times its own weight in water. This moss forms in hummocks in bogs, making a surface where other plants can grow. As new moss forms, it pushes the old moss down underwater, where it decays very slowly, creating a thick blanket of peat. Minnesota peatlands have 164 different kinds of moss.

Labrador tea *Ledum groenlandicum*

The narrow green leaves of Labrador tea stay on the plant year round, so it saves the energy it would require to grow new leaves each year. Its clusters of fragrant white flowers dot the bog, and its leaves have been used to make tea—although drinking too much of this tea can be poisonous.

Leatherleaf *Chamaedaphne calyculata*

Leatherleaf is a low shrub that grows in thick patches in bogs. Its small bell-like flowers hang along the stems. Decaying leatherleaf plants are one of the things that turn bog water brown.

Stemless lady's slipper *Cypripedium acaule*

Lady's slipper orchids grow only when a fungus is present in the soil. This fungus works like root hairs to help the plant absorb nutrients. A lady's slipper may take up to twenty years to flower, and a single cluster of lady's slippers may be one hundred years old.

Bog rosemary *Andromeda glaucophylla*

Bog rosemary's blue-gray leathery leaves roll inward, and its pink flowers hang in clusters from the tips of branches. These flowers spend the winter as buds and open only in the spring.

Round-leaved sundew *Drosera rotundifolia*

Sticky droplets on the hairy, round leaves of these tiny plants trap insects. When the leaf hairs close over a trapped insect, acid slowly dissolves and digests it. Somehow the plants recognize the difference between an insect and a twig or bit of leaf that might fall on them: they only close on and eat the insects.

Pitcher plant *Sarracenia purpurea*

The pitchers of pitcher plants are actually leaves with downward-pointing hairs inside to keep insects that wander in from wandering out again. Down the sides of the pitcher an insect slips, right into the water at the bottom, where it drowns and is slowly digested. Some insects live unharmed in pitcher plants: bog mosquitoes lay their eggs in pitchers, and their larvae survive without being eaten.

Small cranberry *Vaccinium oxycoccus*

Unlike high-bush cranberries, bog cranberries creep along the surface of the bog on trailing stems. The small, bright-red berries are tasty and rich in vitamin C.

Tamarack *Larix laricina*

Tamaracks have needles like other conifer (cone-bearing) trees, but unlike other conifers that keep their needles year round, tamaracks lose their needles every fall and grow new ones every spring. Before the needles fall off, they turn a beautiful golden color.

Black spruce *Picea mariana*

Black spruce is one of the few trees that can grow in bogs. They are tall and scraggly with a distinctive shape: they are thicker at the very top of the tree than just below the top. Their branches can put down new roots where they touch the ground or surface of the moss.

Animals in the Bog

Great gray owl   *Strix nebulosa*

Great gray owls live in peatlands year round and hunt during the day. Their hearing is so acute that they can hear small animals under the snow—and plunge through the snow to catch them.

Palm warbler   *Dendroica palmarum*

Palm warblers are one of the first warblers to return north in the spring. They have a cheery *weeheeheeheeheeheehee ti ti ti* call, and their tails waggle when they walk.

Black-backed woodpecker   *Picoides arcticus*

These birds live year round in and near peatlands, hammering the bark of dead and dying trees to eat the insects under the bark. Their black backs blend with the bark of dying tamaracks and black spruce. They hollow out holes in trees for their nests.

Hermit thrush   *Catharus guttatus*

Hermit thrushes are the first thrushes to arrive in the spring and the last thrushes to migrate in the fall. They fill the bog with their beautiful song. They nest in trees but forage for insects on the ground and in the air.

Sandhill crane   *Grus canadensis*

Sandhill cranes migrate to peatlands to lay their eggs and raise their chicks. Their wings stretch seven feet wide, and when they court each other they do a spectacular dance. Their call sounds like hollow pieces of wood clacking against each other.

Bog copper butterfly
Lycaena epixanthe

The wings of these tiny butterflies are scarcely one inch wide. They lay their eggs on cranberry leaves, where they stay over the winter and hatch in the spring. The caterpillars eat only cranberry leaves and turn into butterflies at the same time that the cranberries flower.

Moose   *Alces alces*

Willow and bog birches provide food for moose in and around the bog. But in Minnesota's Big Bog, most of the moose have mysteriously died off. Scientists don't know why, but some researchers are studying whether a warming climate causes heat stress in moose, which might make the moose more susceptible to parasites and malnutrition.

Woodland caribou   *Rangifer tarandus*

Caribou once ranged across northern Minnesota. The caribou in the Big Bog migrated back and forth along trails to calving grounds in Canada. Settlers, farming, logging, and poaching all contributed to the eventual disappearance of wild caribou from the bog.

Wolf   *Canis lupus*

Because most bog mammals are small, wolves seldom find much food in the bog and usually travel through without hunting.

Bog lemming   *Synaptomys cooperi* and *Synaptomys borealis*

Northern and southern bog lemmings are rarely seen. These four-inch rodents dig nests and tunnels in moss and make stacks of one-inch pieces of grass and sedge to store for food.

Wood frog   *Rana sylvatica*

Wood frogs are "bog frogs," the most common amphibian found in the Big Bog, but even their eggs cannot hatch and grow in the most acidic water. During the winter, wood frogs slowly freeze, but glucose (sugar) in their bodies keeps ice crystals from forming inside the frogs' cells; the crystals only form *between* cells. Come spring, the frogs thaw, unharmed by the cold.

Phyllis Root fell in love with the Big Bog the first time she saw it, mosquitoes and all. She has canoed and kayaked and sailed and river rafted and skied and dogsledded, but the bog is one of the wildest and quietest places she has ever visited. Her other books about nature include *Plant a Pocket of Prairie, One North Star, The Lost Forest,* and *Begin with a Bee.*

Betsy Bowen is the author and illustrator of *Antler, Bear, Canoe: A Northwoods Alphabet Year, Tracks in the Wild,* and *Gathering: A Northwoods Counting Book.* She also illustrated *Plant a Pocket of Prairie, One North Star,* and *The Lost Forest,* all published by the University of Minnesota Press. While she was working on this book, she put on her tallest rubber boots, pocketed her sketchbook and camera, and roamed her northwoods neighborhood bogs, looking at flowers and listening to the birds.